Finding Your Financial Advisor

Finding Your Financial Advisor

HOW TO UNDERSTAND THE INDUSTRY AND CONFIDENTLY HIRE THE BEST

Drew Richey & Shawn Perry

HOUNDSTOOTH

PRESS

FINDING YOUR FINANCIAL ADVISOR

How to Understand the Industry and Confidently Hire the Best

ISBN   978-1-5445-2752-9   *Hardcover*

         978-1-5445-2751-2   *Paperback*

         978-1-5445-2753-6   *Ebook*

Readers of this book should note that it is written with those seeking a full-service, advisory relationship with their financial advisor or financial advisor team in mind. Advisory relationships require a fiduciary standard of care. However, each investor's situation is unique, and advisory services are not always an appropriate avenue. In some cases, a brokerage account may be better suited, especially when considering compensation and needed services. Brokerage services fall outside the fiduciary standard of care but do require financial advisors to satisfy a best-interest standard of care, and brokerage services can still play a vital role in helping investors reach financial goals. When choosing a financial advisor or a financial advisor team, it may be prudent to consider one who is able to provide both advisory services and brokerage services in order to be flexible enough to best meet clients' needs. It is important to understand what you need, what you are paying for, and if your advisor(s) can fulfill those needs wherever they fall on the spectrum of service and product offerings.

The authors of this book are financial advisors, and opinions expressed are solely those of the authors.

All investments carry a level of risk, including loss of principal. Experiences cited in this book may not be representative of the experience of other customers. There is no guarantee that similar outcomes or success will occur in the future.

We dedicate this book to all of the special people who have invested their time, talent, and resources in developing our potential as advisors and men. Thank each of you for selflessly offering wisdom, guidance, and oftentimes, sharing tough love, even when it hurt. Without you all, our business, team, and lives would not be what they are today.

Mike Jennings, "The Founder"

Our Families:

Shawn	**Drew**
Natalie	*Kelsey*
Gavin	*Callie*
Stella Jane	*Jacob*
EmmaLu	

Our Wealth Management Team

Our industry partners, consultants, colleagues, and friends

We love and appreciate you all more than we could ever put in words.

Thank You!

Contents

"If I have seen further it is by
standing on the shoulders of giants."

—ISAAC NEWTON

.

Introduction

"Before anything else, preparation is the key to success."
—ALEXANDER GRAHAM BELL

When people seek financial advice or begin to search for a new financial advisor, it is usually because there has been a transition in their life, and they need help—retirement, the death of a family member, a divorce, or a career or lifestyle change. But there may be a host of other changes that initiate the search for advice. These transitions also come with a wide range of emotions and reactions—from anticipation and celebration, to dread, anxiety, grief, or even paralyzing fear. During these times, the decisions made, and paths chosen, can impact a family's financial legacy for years to come.

If you are currently in one of these transitions, before you decide to work with a financial advisor, you need someone to help you see more clearly, or cut through the noise. You need someone who can help you know, with confidence, what to seek and how to recognize it when you find it. In most cases, people ask friends, family members, or other trusted advisors for recommendations before beginning their search.

Through decades of industry experience and countless engagements with new clients who are working with an advisor for the first time, we've established a core belief in our own practice:

A financial advisor should primarily be, throughout all stages of your engagement, your Financial Advocate.

By definition, an *advocate* is a person who publicly supports or recommends a particular cause or policy. *Advocating* for another person means to plead their case, for their benefit, or on their behalf. This book is written in the spirit of advocating for individuals and families seeking financial advice and assistance with their financial goals, dreams, and needs.

The financial advisor or team you choose can impact your financial well-being for years to come, and there is a lot that should go into that decision.

The financial industry has evolved and continues to change to a level of complexity that makes even the most basic products and services offered hard to understand. We live in the age of information with infinite choices and access to more knowledge and research than we could ever consume. These innovations are mostly positive and can benefit consumers looking for financial advice. Unfortunately, this also creates confusion, uncertainty, and anxiety during a transitionary time in your life that already has its challenges.

The reason for this book is simple:

To help you understand the basics of the retail financial services industry and confidently hire a wealth management team that best suits the current and future needs of your family.

This book is not meant for financial professionals, nor is it for the experts. It is written for regular people who are working toward their own financial goals and seeking help. We will explore the various arrangements you may have with financial advisors, highlight questions you need to ask, and guide you to resources to do your own research. It is our intent that by spending approximately one hour with this guide, you will have the knowledge and understanding to confidently make decisions on how you choose to manage your retirement, wealth, and legacy.

We are committed to changing what people expect from their financial advisor.

The choices for hiring an advisor are wide ranging and varied in scale of services, products, licensing, specialized training, and overall professionalism. People often believe (not by their own fault) that the greatest value advisors can provide is a "unique" financial-planning process or their ability to "beat the market." They have also come to expect a low bar of service, little communication, and reactionary advice.

You should expect more from your financial advisor, and your financial advisor should be giving that to you. You shouldn't have to settle for a reactionary, transactional, product-focused experience when your financial future is at stake, and you truly need advice. It is clear why so many try to do it themselves or seek out the cheapest option possible.

Often, advisors don't provide the value clients expect.

Financial advisory practices should offer a polished, thoughtfully designed, and professional service, just like other trusted professionals you work with. Compare the clinical engagement you have with your physician, the proactive semiannual treatments at the dentist, or even a white-glove, customer-service experience at an upscale restaurant or hotel. These businesses use policy, procedure, planned services, and, most importantly, they show you that you are important and that they care.

We have strategically built our team over three decades to serve the complex needs that investors face today. Our team evolved from a small group of solo practitioners into a multigenerational team of accredited specialists working collaboratively with all our clients. Team members are given clear roles and responsibilities, while processes are implemented to ensure the needs of each client are met. This includes structure around investment management, financial planning, education, ongoing communication, and service. Every part of our engagement with clients, both front- and backstage, is planned, tracked, and repeatable. This consistency in the services we deliver increases confidence, reduces anxiety, and ultimately results in more successful and satisfied clients.

This methodical, planned, yet personal approach to ongoing wealth management means that our clients can anticipate when they will interact with our team both in formal reviews and less formal events. This should be your minimum expectation of the advisor you hire. We want to make that expectation status quo, and this book is about that change.

Whether this is the first time you have been through the hiring process, or you are seeking a new advisor relationship, we want you to have clarity in the options you have, understand what you need to consider, and feel confident in the decision you make.

Thank you for the opportunity to be your Financial Advocate!

PART 1

Taking Ownership

"Honesty is the first chapter in the book of wisdom."

—THOMAS JEFFERSON

Early on as a financial advisor I had an experience in a client meeting that made a lasting impression on me. I was meeting with a gentleman who had left his company in his early fifties. He had retired early and received a substantial amount of money from his company's retirement plan, none of which he contributed himself. In the early years, his investments performed well, but he managed his budget poorly despite our ongoing warnings. He continued spending too much, racking up debt, and eating into the principal of his investments. At the rate he was going, his funds weren't going to last long, and he wasn't even sixty years old. I had to break it to him.

At the pace he was on, he would be completely out of money in five to seven years and not have his debt paid off. He was going bankrupt and couldn't make it stop. After sharing with him again that his financial diagnosis was at a stage three and moving quickly into stage four, he took a pause.

He then looked up, sat forward, and said, "Why didn't anyone tell me this before? How am I supposed to know how to manage this?" As a young financial advisor, I didn't know how to respond.

He continued, "No one ever told me I needed to be preparing for retirement, saving, and learning all of this. They should teach people these things in school." To be honest, I don't even remember how that meeting ended. I do know that he isn't working with our team today, and he eventually ran out of money. It's not an experience I enjoy thinking about, but one I learned a lot from.

Ultimately, we are each responsible for our own actions. When it comes to managing your own financial health and well-being, no one should be more concerned about it than yourself. We must take ownership, and everything that comes with that.

It is true that most people don't have a lot of, if any, formal financial education. High schools now have business and personal finance courses, but this is a newer occurrence. Most people are first introduced to investing in the financial markets through an employer-sponsored retirement plan, such as a 401(k). We find that few are fortunate enough to have had influences in their lives such as a parent, spouse, coworker, or teacher who encouraged them to invest early in life or outside of their workplace retirement plan.

Changes in government regulation, economics, life expectancies, and other factors have caused companies to shift from "guaranteed" retirement plans or pensions to 401(k)s and other types of savings-based plans. Since you are reading this book, we assume you are farther along your financial path and actively seeking advice on how to prepare for your pending retirement, are retired already, or you are in a life transition that requires new advice.

We understand that you are on your own to make these difficult choices, and we know the consequences they carry. Even more so, the impact of the economic and political environment means that the challenges you are facing change often and quickly. Uncertainties exist with taxes, trusts, estate laws, healthcare, insurance needs, stocks and bonds markets, Social Security, inflation, and even longevity.

Let's look at what the research shows.

Did you know that life expectancies are continuing to increase, and if you are sixty-five years old, the chances of living to a ripe old age are high? In fact, the probability of a sixty-five-year-old couple having at least one spouse living to age ninety is nearly 50 percent.

If you're 65 today, the probability of living to a specific age or beyond

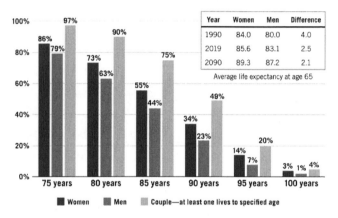

Source (chart): Social Security Administration, Period Life Table, 2017 (published in 2020), J.P. Morgan Asset Management.
Source (table): Social Security Administration 2020 OASDI Trustees Report.
Probability at least one member of a same-sex female couple lives to age 90 is 56% and a same-sex male couple is 40%.

Additionally, spending habits generally shift over our lifetimes, often into areas that see high rates of inflation. In fact, the cost of healthcare has historically experienced higher inflation than other categories and is where retirees often see a large increase in spending.

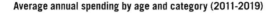

Average annual spending by age and category (2011-2019)

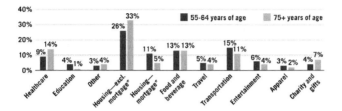

Average inflation by spending category (1982-2020)

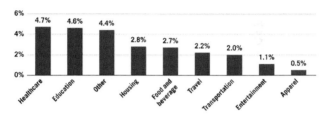

*There are no individual inflation measures for these specific subcategories.

Source (top chart): BLS, 2017-2019 annuall average Consumer Expenditure Survey for households where at least one member has a bachelor's degree. Charitable contributions include girfts to religious, educational and political organizations, and other cash gifts. Spending percentages may not equal 100% due to rounding.

Source (bottom chart): BLS, Consumer Price Index, J.P. Morgan Asset Management. Data represent annual percentage increase from December 1981 through December 2020 with the exception of entertainment and education, which date back to 1993, and travel, which dates back to 2001. The inflation rate for the Other category is derived from personal care products and tobacco. Tobacco has experienced 7% inflation since 1986.

There is clearly a need to invest and make the assets you have accumulated work for you. Savings accounts, money markets, CDs, and insurance products alone aren't likely to keep up, but investing in the financial markets can be risky. This is why you need to be educated.

Becoming an educated investor and understanding the relationship between risk and reward—and using this as a means to accomplishing your personal and financial goals—can be a lifelong journey. The capital markets are complex and usually don't move in a straight line. The markets have their ups and downs and can sometimes feel like a roller coaster. While this book isn't about understanding how to navigate the capital markets and become a seasoned investor, this section is about helping you understand why it is so important to choose a partner who can guide you.

Here's what's at stake.

The stock markets fluctuate and have corrections, dips, pull-backs, and crashes. However you describe it, almost every week, in good markets and in bad, people ask if we foresee a market decline. So, what do we tell them?

Here's what the statistics show.

On average, for over forty years, the market experiences annual intrayear declines in excess of 14 percent but ends positive nearly 75 percent of the time.

S&P 500 intra-year declines vs. calendar year returns
Despite average intra-year drops of 14.3%, annual returns were positive in 31 of 41 years

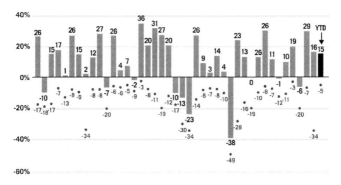

Source: FactSet, Standard & Poor's, J.P. Morgan Asset Management. Returns are based on price index only and do not include dividends. Intra-year drops refers to the largest market drops from a peak to a trough during the year. For illustrative purposes only. Returns shown are calendar year returns from 1980 to 2020, over which time period the average annual return was 9.0%. Guide to the Markets—U.S. Data are as of September 30, 2021.

So, answer the question for yourself. If this is the average annual decline for over forty years, is the stock market going to decline soon? Sure, it happens almost every year. It's completely normal.

The next assumption is often this.

If the market declines every year, why shouldn't we just *get out* when it starts, and then get back in when it's over? Another version of this is "Why don't we just time the market?" The impact of trying to time the market can mean risking your family's livelihood for the long term. In fact, even over long periods of time, most of your investment returns are likely to come from just a small number of days.

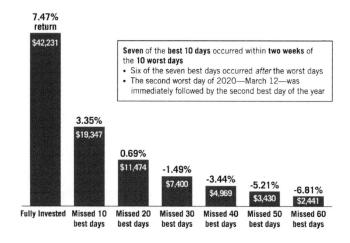

Returns of the S&P 500
Performance of a $10,000 investment between January 2, 2001 and December 31, 2020

Seven of the **best 10 days** occurred within **two weeks** of the **10 worst days**
- Six of the seven best days occurred *after* the worst days
- The second worst day of 2020—March 12—was immediately followed by the second best day of the year

	7.47% return	3.35%	0.69%	-1.49%	-3.44%	-5.21%	-6.81%
	$42,231	$19,347	$11,474	$7,400	$4,969	$3,430	$2,441
	Fully Invested	Missed 10 best days	Missed 20 best days	Missed 30 best days	Missed 40 best days	Missed 50 best days	Missed 60 best days

Source: J.P. Morgan Asset Management analysis using data from Bloomberg. Returns are based on the S&P 500 Total Return Index, an unmanaged, capitalization-weighted index that measures the performance of 500 large capitalization domestic stocks representing all major industries. Indices do not include fees or operating expenses and are not available for actual investment. The hypothetical performance calculations are shown for illustrative purposes only and are not meant to be representative of actual results while investing over the time periods shown. The hypothetical performance calculations are shown gross of fees. If fees were included, returns would be lower. Hypothetical performance returns reflect the reinvestment of all dividends. The hypothetical performance results have certain inherent limitations. Unlike an actual performance record, they do not reflect actual trading, liquidity constraints, fees and other costs. Also, since the trades have not actually been executed, the results may have under- or overcompensated for the impact of certain market factors such as lack of liquidity. Simulated trading programs in general are also subject to the fact that they are designed with the benefit of hindsight. Returns will fluctuate and an investment upon redemption may be worth more or less than its original value. Past performance is not indicative of future returns. An individual cannot invest directly in an index. Data as of December 31, 2020.

Unfortunately, those best days that generate most of your returns often come close to the worst days. When do you think people sell out of their investments or try to "time the market"?

Furthermore, the potential gain from timing your investment decisions with fluctuations of the markets offers much less opportunity than most people realize. A recent study by Russell Investments shows that investment returns from great timing compared to poor timing only marginally increase, even over a long time period.

Hypothetical ending wealth after investing $12,000 per year
Period ending December 31, 2020

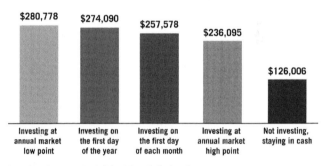

| $280,778 | $274,090 | $257,578 | $236,095 | $126,006 |

| Investing at annual market low point | Investing on the first day of the year | Investing on the first day of each month | Investing at annual market high point | Not investing, staying in cash |

Source: Russell Investments. Hypothetical analysis provided for illustrative purposes only.

Indexes are unmanaged and cannot be invested in directly. Returns represent past performance, are not a guarantee of future performance, and are not indicative of any specific investment.

Note: One year represents a 12-month period ending December 31.

Assumes an investment of $12,000 per year into a hypothetical S&P 500 Index portfolio with no withdrawals between Jan 1, 2011 and Dec 31, 2020.

Cash return based on return of $12,000 invested each year in a hypothetical portfolio of 3 month Treasury bonds represented by the FTSE Treasury Bill

3-month Index without any withdrawals between Jan 31, 2011 and Dec 31, 2020.

Since the burden of navigating these uncertainties and managing your transition falls solely on you, many seek help. This may come in the form of resources available online, advice from family or colleagues, or by hiring a financial services firm. If you were going to build a house, you would hire a builder and start with a plan.

Similarly, it is wise to hire an experienced professional who helps people with the same challenges you are facing.

What does it mean to hire a financial advisor?

Hiring a financial advisor can mean contracting someone to build a financial plan for a flat fee, but more traditionally it refers to an engagement with an individual or group that provides ongoing financial advice and services. However, there are so many different options available to you as an investor that it can be hard to know exactly what type of help you really need. People often look to others who have some experience or are more familiar with how to make these decisions. They research online and talk to multiple advisors but still feel confused about what else may be out there or what they may be missing. This combined with thousands of different investment products plus dozens of cost structures can cause anxiety and be overwhelming.

Most people are left frustrated and wonder why it has to be so complicated.

The Industry of Advice

The financial services industry can seem so complex that it is easy to be skeptical of the entire process. Why are there so many firms?

What are the differences between them? How does someone even become a financial advisor?

The financial advisor title itself implies attainment of specialized knowledge, licenses, and credentials that qualifies someone to give financial advice to others. Think of it this way: we know that an accountant who is a CPA has attained an esteemed, higher level of expertise; an attorney passed the bar exam and became licensed to practice law; a physician went to medical school. But what, exactly, are the requirements to earn the title of financial advisor?

Often, a financial advisor was simply hired as a salesperson at their company to open new accounts and find new clients. Others may have started their own practice and labeled themselves a financial advisor or may have only completed something as basic as a state life insurance licensing exam. There are plenty of inexperienced salespeople tasked with the goal of opening a specific number of accounts each month or selling a certain number of life insurance policies. In many cases, they may be pushing specific (and likely expensive) products or insurance on every client who uses their company for tax preparation or banking services.

Does this truly describe a financial advisor?

If you talk with someone who seems to fit any of the following general categories, you can be sure they are not what you are looking for:

- The Annuity Salesman

- The Life Insurance Company Representative

- The Tax Preparer Advisor

- The Product Pusher

The easiest way to describe these types of arrangements is that the interaction feels more like a transaction than a relationship. There is a beginning and an end with little or no ongoing advice. In comparison, working with a true financial advisor should provide a more meaningful engagement: seeking first to understand you and your goals, implementing cost-efficient strategies and solutions, and providing ongoing monitoring and adjustments.

Government oversight in the industry has helped regulate some of this by placing higher standards of care on professionals who truly serve as advisors. This legal standard of care is known as the "fiduciary standard." By definition, a *fiduciary* is someone who is held or founded in trust or confidence. It could be difficult for a financial advisor who has product sales goals, lacks industry certifications and professional certifications, or sells only their company products to be described as "held or founded in trust or confidence." Their conflicts of interest are too great.

It is widely assumed that there is a legal standard that all financial professionals are held to, but that is not the case.

Not all advisors work under the same standard of care. Some are only held to a suitability standard, meaning that recommendations must be suited to, but not necessarily in, a client's best interest. Others still have even less responsibility to their clients and more to their company.

Based on everything covered in this section, it should now be clear why you must take ownership of your own success. The stakes are high, the challenge is difficult, and the path you choose matters. That is why you owe it to yourself to be informed.

You must know the right questions to ask, what to look for, and what your options are.

Where do you start?

PART 2

Defining Your Minimum Standards

"Hiring the best is your most important task."

—STEVE JOBS

Now that you have a clearer understanding of how the industry works and some of the most common pitfalls you should avoid, let's discuss selecting the right partner for you and your family. Doing your research prior to meeting with an advisor can help you save time and determine exactly what you are looking for. To help with this process, we have developed a *Pre-Meeting Checklist* with key elements for you to understand and identify in regard to any advisor you are considering. You can download this from our website (www.findingyourfinancialadvisor.com) and print as many copies as you need. This will set the baseline for your Five Minimum Standards.

There are *Five Minimum Standards* that you need to understand before you begin interviews with financial advisors.

Remember, these are the baseline minimums or barriers to an advisor getting an interview with you. If they can't check *all* of these boxes, they likely aren't worth your consideration. There are lots of advisors who meet all of these, so there should not be a need to lower your standards for anyone. They are as follows:

- Education

- Background Check

- Services Offered

- Practice Profile

- Cost

The following section outlines each of these in detail and will help you narrow your search and begin interviews.

Education

ARE THEY AN EXPERT?

The financial services industry has less stringent barriers to entry than many other professional services. For example, you can trust that a tax preparer who is a CPA has more advanced knowledge and training than one who is not, and you know an attorney was required to obtain a law degree and pass the bar exam. However, the range of education and training for someone to serve as a financial advisor may be as low as passing a state insurance licensing exam or as high as a PhD with multiple professional certifications. There are many notable educational programs, university degrees, and professional certifications in the field, but one stands out from the rest.

The CERTIFIED FINANCIAL PLANNER™ certification is considered the benchmark of the industry and clearly demonstrates competency and professionalism. To obtain this distinction, an individual must have a bachelor's degree from an accredited university or college, complete a financial education curriculum, have a minimum amount of experience, pass a rigorous exam, enter into an ethics agreement, and satisfy an ongoing continuing education and recertification program. Additionally, a requirement of all CFP® professionals is the requirement to adhere to a code of ethics that maintains the fiduciary standard as we discussed in Part 1.

Here is how the CFP® Board describes their certification:

Plan with Confidence. Partner with a CFP® Professional.

When it comes to your financial security, it's all about partnering with someone who is committed to putting your interests first. CFP® professionals have attained the standard of excellence in financial planning by meeting education, experience, and ethical standards, and as part of their certification, they have made a commitment to the CFP® Board to serve your best interests today to prepare you for a more secure tomorrow.[1]

There certainly are other esteemed programs, certifications, and credentials, but this should be the minimum standard to earn an interview with you.

You can learn more about this specific certificate on the CFP®
website at www.letsmakeaplan.org.

Remember, all certifications are not created equal, and there are
many that can be acquired with very minimal effort and little to
no continuing education. Aside from the CERTIFIED FINANCIAL
PLANNER™ certification, the Investments and Wealth Institute®
(www.investmentsandwealth.org) offers two highly advanced,
specialized certifications that are very prominent in the financial
services industry.

The Investments and Wealth Institute® describes them like this:

CPWA® or Certified Private Wealth Advisor®

Certified Private Wealth Advisor® (CPWA®) is an advanced
professional certification for advisors who serve high-net-
worth clients. It's designed for seasoned professionals who
seek the latest, most advanced knowledge and techniques
to address the sophisticated needs of clients with a minimum net worth of five million dollars. Unlike credentials
that focus specifically on investing or financial planning,
the CPWA® program takes a holistic and multidisciplinary
approach.[2]

CIMA® or Certified Investment Management Analyst®

Certified Investment Management Analyst® (CIMA®) certification is the peak international, technical portfolio construction program for investment consultants, analysts, financial advisors, and wealth management professionals. CIMA® certification continues to be the highest level of advanced investment education for client-facing advisors.[3]

If you find a team or an advisor who has multiple certifications, then that will most certainly demonstrate a commitment to excellence.

Background Check

TRUST BUT VERIFY

The retail financial services industry is highly regulated by two primary organizations: Financial Industry Regulatory Authority® (FINRA®) and the US Securities and Exchange Commission (SEC). Following is a short description of each organization as shown on their respective websites:

FINRA®—Financial Industry Regulatory Authority®[4]

Every investor in America relies on one thing: fair financial markets. To protect investors and ensure the market's integrity, FINRA® is a government-authorized not-for-profit organization that oversees U.S. broker-dealers. We work every day to ensure that everyone can participate in the market with confidence.

- every investor receives the basic protections they deserve;

- anyone who sells a securities product has been tested, qualified and licensed;

- every securities product advertisement used is truthful, and not misleading;

- any securities product sold to an investor is suitable for that investor's needs; and

- investors receive complete disclosure about the investment product before purchase.

US Securities and Exchange Commission (SEC)[5]

At the Securities and Exchange Commission (SEC), we work together to make a positive impact on America's economy, our capital markets, and people's lives.

For more than 85 years since our founding at the height of the Great Depression, we have stayed true to our mission of protecting investors, maintaining fair, orderly, and efficient markets, and facilitating capital formation.

Our mission requires tireless commitment and unique expertise from our staff of dedicated professionals who care deeply about protecting Main Street investors and others who rely on our markets to secure their financial futures.

Learn more about specific SEC functions and responsibilities carried out by various divisions and offices within our Washington DC headquarters and 11 regional offices around the country

These organizations provide publicly available resources you can access to help research an advisor or team you may be interested in interviewing. Employment, licensing, and disciplinary history for financial industry professionals can be found on their respective websites. We have included these in the resources listed in the back of this book.[6,7] If the advisor you are vetting is not found on these websites, it means they don't carry the license necessary to be regulated through these organizations. This should be a red flag.

Most advisors have an online presence where much of this information is easily accessed. Spend some time searching for information about them, their team, and their firm. These days everyone has a digital footprint, and it is worth investigating.

Services Offered

THE TRUTH ABOUT FINANCIAL PLANNING

Since the early 1990s, the industry has shifted from primarily offering transactional investment services to a more advice-based engagement where other services are often the focus. Today, financial planning is now offered by most advisors, though a financial plan may range anywhere from a basic snapshot to a comprehensive wealth management engagement. A snapshot plan provides a simplified present view of your financial picture and is typically accompanied by action steps of what you need to do to accomplish current, specific goals. These may include funding emergency savings accounts, retirement savings plans, retirement income projections, investment recommendations, insurance, and liability planning. This is usually done for a fee and typically includes recommendations to buy several types of products from the advisor.

On the other end of the spectrum, a comprehensive approach to planning includes all of the above but will be monitored and adjusted on an ongoing basis. These adjustments are based on the implementation of your plan and the actual results of how you are tracking toward your goals. Life changes occur often and sometimes suddenly, and it will be necessary to update things from time to time. This type of planning allows for that and is usually included in the cost of ongoing investment management.

If you come across a financial advisor who doesn't offer at least minimal basic planning, it's probably not worth interviewing them at all.

A lot of financial advisors talk about their financial planning process as if it's something unique to their practice or really sets them apart from their competition. There are different types of planning tools and a range of focuses they can address. A plan may range from an in-depth tax analysis to a basic retirement income plan.

The truth about the financial planning process is this:

It is not, *and should not be*, a unique process.

The financial planning process is simply a series of prudent steps identified over several decades, verified by academia and the real world, that helps clients make better decisions with their money.

In fact, the CFP® Board outlines a defined seven-step process every CFP® practitioner should use in working with clients.

Step 1: Understand the Client's Personal and Financial Circumstances

Step 2: Identifying and Selecting Goals

Step 3: Analyzing the Client's Current Course of Action and Potential Alternative Course(s) of Action

Step 4: Developing the Financial Planning Recommendation(s)

Step 5: Presenting the Financial Planning Recommendation(s)

Step 6: Implementing the Financial Planning Recommendation(s) (Unless Specifically Excluded from Scope of Engagement)

Step 7: Monitoring Progress and Updating (Unless Specifically Excluded from Scope of Engagement)

Additionally, there are clear guidelines defining why a step may be omitted and how to disclose that. You can learn more about what the CFP® Board says regarding the financial planning process directly on their website. We have included the link to their code of ethics, which details all of this, on the Resources page in the back of this book.[8]

As a quick exercise, search "financial planning process" online, and you can see that the process is certainly not unique. The point here is that the planning process is mostly standardized and should be dealt with as such.

Practice Profile

SOLO ADVISORS VERSUS A TEAM

About the same time financial advisors began offering basic financial planning services, the industry began to shift from individual financial advisors to a more team-based approach. Historically, a seasoned advisor would hire a younger advisor with a college degree in financial planning or something similar, and the practice would begin to evolve. These early teams began to separate responsibilities and offer new services to differentiate their practices and more meaningfully help clients.

If you are interviewing a solo advisor, think long and hard about how a single advisor could offer you competitive services compared to a team.

For instance, who is there to help you when the advisor is away from the office, traveling, or busy with other clients? Do they have a succession plan, or will you be left to search for a new advisor when they retire? Worse yet, will you just be handed off to someone else within their firm?

On the contrary, if there is a team in place, it's important to know that not all teams are created equal.

Some teams operate more like a group of individuals who provide backup coverage for one another. They may share resources, space, and even administrative staff for their own financial benefit. It does not necessarily mean they work together to better serve their clients.

Think of it like this:

Are they more like a golf team, where the golfers play individually and total their scores at the end of the round, or a basketball team, which functions as one collaborative unit with each member playing their own position, each being vital to the game?

There are many comprehensive wealth-management teams that have numerous advisors with varying specialties and specialized education to serve clients. Most are multigenerational and can provide solutions for all of these issues solo practitioners are unable to address. The industry has evolved well past solo practitioners.

If there is not a strategically built, multigenerational team of specialists in place to support your financial needs, it's probably best to keep looking.

Costs

HOW DO THEY GET PAID?

As practices evolved and changed the way they served clients and grew their businesses, they began shifting from a commission-based, transactional cost structure to charging ongoing fees for continued advice and monitoring. Some advisors work with firms that accommodate a combination of both options for clients. There are many ways an advisor may charge clients, with most firms giving advisor teams the freedom to customize how they structure costs.

The three most common types of cost structures are:

1. Asset-based fee

    › A percentage cost, based on the value of your investments.

2. Fee for service

    › A flat rate charge for specific services provided.

3. Transactional

    › A commission charge per transaction to buy or sell securities or other products.

    › Ongoing internal expenses may also exist in products purchased through commissions or sales charges.

    › These may include additional compensation for the advisor that a lot of clients are surprised to learn about.

All of these can be prudent options and may be appropriate given your goals or preferences.

Independent of how this is structured, it is most important to make sure that how you pay your wealth-management team is entirely transparent and aligns with your goals.

Do you want ongoing services and planning year after year

throughout retirement, or do you want someone to help set things up and send you on your way? Do you want ongoing investment monitoring and adjustments, or advice on how to structure your account and then you take it from there? You are the only one who can answer these questions; just be sure you understand which makes the most sense for you and your family.

Final Interview Preparation

Now that you have narrowed your list of prospective advisors by education, background check, services provided, team profile, and preferred cost structure, you are ready to begin scheduling interviews. Remember, this industry is complicated, and you need to take your time to get it right. You should not risk working with anyone whose primary business is anything other than providing financial advice for people like you. Advisors may have different specialties, such as retirement income planning or assisting through specific types of transitions. It's also worth mentioning that you do not want to be anyone's largest, most complex client. Similar to working with a surgeon who has repeated a procedure thousands of times before, you want to find an advisor who focuses on helping people just like you.

The initial interview meeting is a time for you to familiarize yourself with the team you are considering, for them to get to know you, and to see if your goals align with what they provide.

People often wonder what they need to bring to a first meeting. The answer is simple: only your list of questions.

You haven't hired them yet, so there is no need to share financial statements or paperwork for them to review. There will be plenty of time for that if you decide to hire them. This meeting is about the discovery process and determining whether they are the best fit. If their process begins with anything other than getting to know you and discussing how they can serve you, then that may tell you all you need to know.

What should you be looking for in your interviews?

PART 3

The Interviews

"If you think it's expensive to hire a professional,
wait until you hire an amateur."

—RED ADAIR

It should now be clear that having the education, background, team, range of services and products, and fair costs are simply the status quo. These are your Five Minimum Standards. An advisor cannot get an interview with you unless they meet each of these. So, what separates excellence from mediocrity? A true, professional wealth-management team does much more than meet minimum expectations.

When you find the right fit, you will feel confident, comfortable, and connected with who you choose to serve you and the plan they have helped you build.

This involves much more than knowledge and skills. The wealth-management team you choose should utilize a Core Value approach.

A Core Value Approach to Wealth Management

A comprehensive and ongoing wealth-management experience can be categorized into four main Core Values:

- Wisdom

- Discipline

- Transparency

- Humility

These Core Values establish the foundation for your interviews, since the team you are meeting with has already gotten past your initial vetting process and has met your Five Minimum Standards. At this point, everything you will want to learn about your prospective advisor team falls into these four categories. Be sure to take our *Advisor Interview Questionnaire* (available at www.findingyourfinancialadvisor.com) to your meeting for easy reference and note-taking.

Wisdom

"Where there is no counsel, the people fall;
but in the multitude of counselors there is safety."

—PROVERBS 11:14

Education, proper licensing, and professional certifications are prerequisites to earning your business. But what does it mean to apply that knowledge through Wisdom? There are three key components you should look for:

- Specialization within the Team

- Coordination with Other Professionals

- Client Education Program

SPECIALIZATION WITHIN THE TEAM

Having a team is necessary, but how do they work together? Advisor teams form for a multitude of reasons, some of which can be more beneficial to the advisors themselves than the clients they serve. Recall our example from Part 2 about a basketball team compared to a golf team.

A high-performing team differentiates roles and areas of specialty among their team members, and they each are there to serve a unique role for their clients. You should interact with multiple team members before you meet for the first time. You can ask targeted questions to quickly help you identify if their team is built to provide more for you, or for them:

- Will I be working with the other members of your team?

- How do I know who to call with questions or service needs?

- Will I meet with more than one advisor?

- Do the advisors have different areas of specialization?

- Who do I call if you are not available?

- What will happen to my accounts if something happens to you?

If your first meeting is with the advisor only, then their "team" may be more coverage for their time away, sharing of service staff, or planning for their own retirement than truly a team of experts built for your benefit.

Be sure to take note of who attends and participates in your first meeting.

COORDINATION WITH OTHER PROFESSIONALS

The saying "It takes a village" applies in more ways than one when it comes to navigating your retirement. The advisor team you choose should have a complete network of other service professionals to assist them in advising you.

A few years back, we had a long-term client pass away who was the primary family member consistently engaged in the family's wealth management and financial planning. His spouse wasn't actively involved, and now she was left to sort things out.

Thankfully we had helped our deceased client put an entire network of trusted advisors in place. He was one of the largest clients we had ever worked with, and we went to great lengths to educate ourselves on his advanced planning needs and coordinate every resource possible. We had helped coordinate establishing an estate plan with the family's attorney, implemented tax-efficient investment strategies with their CPA, and became the sounding board for the family.

Shortly after the funeral, we facilitated a meeting with all of these trusted advisors. Several of our key team members were involved as well as the CPA we had connected the family with, their estate attorney, our client's widow, and their adult children. Over the course of this meeting and several follow-up sessions, we were able to develop a plan for the family to move forward. Recommendations were made and strategies were seamlessly executed. Driving home that day, I remember thinking how beneficial this collaboration was for our client and her family for years to come. Following this experience, we made it our standard of care that every family has that structure in place. Coordination among our clients' other trusted advisors is now commonplace in our practice.

Helping connect you with other professionals and coordinating with your other trusted advisors should be a part of the process, not something you have to request.

They should be able to anticipate needs you are not yet aware of, have had other clients with similar needs, and have access to helpful outside resources. These should include the following:

- Estate planning attorneys

- CPAs and tax preparers

- Medicare consultants

- Insurance advisors

- Real estate professionals

- Travel agents

- Counselors

- Coaches

This should be discussed at the first meeting since it is a major part of the value an advisor team can provide. They should be actively involved in their community and networking with all of these service providers to benefit their clients. Ask questions to understand how they stay involved and up-to-date with other professionals, and what networks they have that can benefit you. This is a key indicator of their ability to be proactive, anticipate needs their clients may have, and offer solutions.

The value of this is often overlooked but adds significantly to the benefits of working with the right team.

CLIENT EDUCATION PROGRAM

There are many factors that come into play during the course of your financial life. Some of these we have full control over, some partial control, and others no control. For this reason, it's crucial that education be an important component of your engagement with your advisor team. Having an understanding of capital markets, economics, legislation, and the timeless principles of investing are crucial to your long-term success. Perhaps even more importantly, understanding these external factors directly impacts your comfort level and ability to stick with your financial plan over a long period of time. You want to work with an advisor team who understands this and goes to great lengths to keep you informed. A strategically built, diverse, multimedia educational program will provide a variety of ways to keep you educated and informed:

- Advisor team podcasts

- Newsletters and e-newsletters

- Quarterly practice updates

- Investor and capital market communications

- Annual review meetings

- Topical seminars

- Regular phone interactions

If this is a foundational part of their service component, they will tell you about it. If they don't, be sure to ask how you can expect to be kept informed.

Discipline

"Discipline is the bridge between
goals and accomplishment."

—JIM ROHN

There are simply too many moving parts to comprehensive wealth management to leave any aspect of it to chance or discretion. There are a multitude of ways to manage this, but it is important there is a process or series of checklists in place. Every member of an advisor team should be able to articulate these core components, and resources should be provided to help you understand them. This will be multifaceted, but you can get a feel for their Disciplined approach by asking questions about the following:

- The Wealth-Management Process

- The Investment Process

- The Standard of Care and Client Advocacy

- Ongoing Service and Communication

THE WEALTH-MANAGEMENT PROCESS

Having a Disciplined wealth-management process is a baseline for a professional team. This is more comprehensive than the financial planning process, but it should be clearly articulated and obvious that this is second nature to their team.

You should be concerned if this process begins with anything other than understanding your priorities and goals.

Unless you have specific questions, reviewing your statements and discussing products should be several steps into the process and should not be a part of your first meeting.

Everything this entails begins when you commit to working with a team and will likely take several meetings to accomplish. Asking questions about their process is different than beginning the process with them at your first meeting. The point is to make sure they have a carefully designed, well-thought-out process that they work through to understand you before making specific recommendations.

THE INVESTMENT PROCESS

There are hundreds, if not thousands, of investment strategies, platforms, and products that all may lead you to the same end result. This is not about what products they use but about having a Disciplined approach to investing.

- How many different strategies do they use?

- How do they monitor, evaluate, and adjust?

- Do their clients utilize similar strategies, or is each one customized?

- How do they control and minimize the less visible, internal investment costs?

The actual investment strategy they implement may be less important than having one that is thought out, easily articulated, and repeatable. For example, if you're told that each client's portfolio is completely customized, it's likely that there isn't a preexisting investment process established. Again, there are many suitable strategies, but you need to ask questions to understand their approach and make sure it aligns with your goals. You don't need to fully comprehend all the factors that go into building investment portfolios to feel confident asking questions. Your goal here is to gain an understanding of how Disciplined their approach is.

- How do they balance portfolios among different asset classes?

  › Stocks versus bonds

  › Large versus small companies

  › US versus international

- Do they use professional money managers, mutual funds, exchange traded funds (ETFs), or pick individual securities themselves?

  › Active versus passive investing

- Is their investment philosophy more strategic or tactical?

  › Long-term or short-term horizon

- Will there be a lot of turnover or trading?

- How often do they rebalance portfolios?

- How do they plan for client withdrawals/income planning?

- How do they implement investment strategies?

  › Dollar-cost averaging

These questions are all found in your *Advisor Interview Questionnaire* and on our website (www.findingyourfinancialadvisor.com) so you can have them with you at your meeting.

THE STANDARD OF CARE AND CLIENT ADVOCACY

At any given point in your journey as an investor, there are a number of topics that will need to be addressed. Your advisor team should proactively identify and address these through ongoing, regular review meetings and their client-education curriculum.

A standard of care approach to wealth management helps ensure that the right things are addressed at the right time.

The issues you face now are different than the issues you will face in twenty years. Just as your doctor goes through a certain protocol for tests and exams when you reach certain ages, your wealth-management team should have a process for addressing certain topics as you reach major milestones. They should use a series of checklists to identify issues people face throughout their financial lives, from education planning to caring for aging parents. Otherwise, it would be easy, and even likely, for something to slip through the cracks.

An advisor team can only truly be your Financial Advocate if their primary goal is to help identify and address all of the challenges you and your family will face throughout your life.

To implement this elevated standard of care, they will likely have key team members dedicated to this role. Just as your doctor has a team to run tests, ask questions, and assist with preparation and follow-up, there should be dedicated team members who partner with a client's primary advisor to fulfill the standard of care. This will ensure your needs are being met. This may be the single most important differentiator of a team with whom you want to work.

ONGOING SERVICE AND COMMUNICATION

Communication is key to any relationship, and that is no different with your advisor team. Communications with you, including regular updates on the capital markets and economics, news that impacts your strategies and investments, and any other need-to-know information should be planned and predictable. Personalized reviews of your planning and investment strategies should be regularly scheduled as well. Communications to you should come in many forms and be often and consistent.

Perhaps even more important is their ability to connect with you during times of uncertainty, anxiety, and extreme market volatility.

We discussed in Part 1, "Taking Ownership," the impact of abandoning your strategies during volatile markets. Morgan Housel says it best in his book *The Psychology of Money*: "Your success as an investor is determined by how you respond to punctuated moments of terror, not the years spent on cruise control."[9]

During the extreme volatility of the Great Recession of 2008–2009, our team spent every day contacting as many clients as possible. Our intent was to reassure them we were present, monitoring the climate, and ready to help them if there was a need. In times such as this, there is a need to recommit to the strategies and plans you've put in place, and not lose sight of the long-term impact that a knee-jerk reaction could have.

During this time, by chance, there happened to be three families of our clients vacationing together, and a fourth couple with them we did not work with. As we touched base on nearly a weekly basis, they mentioned that their friends still had not heard from their advisor. They appreciated our communications and reassurance even more because of this. The couple who never heard from their own advisor still had some comfort in the steadfast message we were communicating to their friends.

As you can imagine, the fourth couple who never heard from their advisor was frustrated, insecure, and realized this lack of contact was unacceptable. The week after they returned from their trip, they set an appointment and came to our office with those same travel companions. They met with our team, transferred their accounts, and are still clients to this day. These are the times when it's easy to lose sight of your long-term plan and act out of fear.

Can you expect to hear from the advisor team directly when these events occur?

When you work with a sophisticated wealth management team, they will have many clients. They will have systems and processes to ensure these communications are timely and happen efficiently. Ask questions to understand how they plan to communicate and serve you on an ongoing basis.

Transparency

"Transparency is the currency of trust."

—UNKNOWN

Transparency within a wealth management practice falls into four main categories:

- Costs and Fees

- Open Firm Architecture

- Insights into Decision-Making

- The Company They Work With

COSTS AND FEES

We discussed this earlier, but it is so important that it is worth mentioning again. Transparency as a Core Value establishes the basis for trust in your relationship. There is no clearer example than transparency of costs.

There are numerous examples of hidden fees or costs in other industries that you are familiar with. Hotels have cleaning fees, airlines have baggage fees, and most investments have internal fees. Make sure that all costs are disclosed up front to you, preferably without you having to inquire about them. There are four main costs that should be disclosed to you before ever opening an account:

- Advisory fees

- Manager expenses

- Firm and account charges

- Internal investment costs

It may be the case that not all of these apply, or there may be broader charges that cover multiple expenses. It is crucial that there is clear communication, full Transparency, and that you understand it entirely. This makes it easy to compare those costs to industry averages with other investors similar to you. These details should be easily provided to you upon request.

OPEN FIRM ARCHITECTURE

This is a complicated term that describes the advisor team's relationship with their firm and how they choose and implement investment options. *Open* means they have access to most of the major options that are available on the open markets. *Closed* means they are much more limited to what they can offer and generally only have access to proprietary options or those specific to their firm. There may be investment strategies or products only available within their firm that are entirely appropriate. It is important to ensure they are high quality, cost efficient, and that there is no ulterior motive (think "kickbacks") for them to recommend to you.

INSIGHTS INTO DECISION-MAKING

Ideally, the team you select will provide opportunities for education and interaction throughout the process. It is important to understand how they monitor your accounts and strategies month to month, how they organize and manage their business, and how they interact together as a team. A team should communicate frequently in a variety of ways to offer clients direct insights into what is going on within their business, their observations in the capital markets, and what clients need to know to stay up-to-date.

Every part of your advisor team's processes should be visible and communicated to you.

Nothing about this should be a trade secret or something they don't want to discuss. If they shy away from this, their processes likely lack Discipline and Transparency, which should raise concern.

THE COMPANY THEY WORK WITH

The financial services firm your team works with greatly impacts how they serve you. A team depends on their firm to provide valuable resources to them and their clients. Technology, research, investment platforms, reporting systems, industry specialists, and regulatory oversight are just a few key aspects where a firm can either greatly enhance or hinder a team.

The highly regulated compliance protocols and increased fiduciary responsibility make having an independent advisor or one that is not affiliated with a larger firm much less attractive. Regulatory oversight, compliance and reporting requirements, and the complexity of trading and investment platforms mean that no team is truly independent of a larger support system or firm backing.

A reputable firm will provide the advisor team with a plethora of resources to serve clients, systems to manage investment and service processes, and they'll give you peace of mind that regulatory requirements are being met. As a client, your experience can ultimately be enhanced by the firm you select.

Humility

> "True humility is not thinking less of yourself;
> it is thinking of yourself less."
> —RICK WARREN

Humility is perhaps the least tangible of the primary Core Values a wealth management team should possess. Technically, there are products sold to clients, but this is a service and hospitality business. Think of experiences you have had with businesses where you felt they were honored to serve you or made you feel more like they were doing you a favor. This is more of a "you know it when you see it" value, but there are ways to identify if it is something your potential advisors embrace. This part of your conversation focuses on three main elements:

- Relationships

- Community

- Gratitude and Appreciation

RELATIONSHIPS

You need to feel connected to the people with whom you are working. They should take the time to get to know you and understand your unique goals and circumstances. Your business, no matter how large or small, is unique and should be treated that way. The importance of being understood and the engagement being centered around your personal needs cannot be stressed enough.

As an advisor team's client base gets larger, it will be harder for them to maintain quality, relationship-focused service.

It's likely necessary that in order to maintain this, an advisor team will need to implement account minimums, limit the number of clients they serve, or grow their team.

Ask questions to understand what standards they have in order to maintain their quality of service. It is usually not hard to tell if you are more of a number than a person. This culture will resonate with every member of the team and how they interact with you.

COMMUNITY

When businesses serve their community, they become a part of something bigger. The community your team serves extends further than their client base and is part of the town, state, and region they serve. Through this community, they connect more deeply with other centers of influence, businesses, and resources to better serve you and all their clients. Offering resources, education, and other opportunities to businesses and professionals in their network greatly expands their ability to serve you.

GRATITUDE AND APPRECIATION

Gratitude is the quality of being thankful, and *appreciation* means to recognize something's full worth. In our industry, we find that gratitude and appreciation are shown in two primary ways.

The first is through a contact, event, or opportunity to connect with you on a meaningful personal level. This may be as simple as a phone call to check on you, a greeting card recognizing a special day, or a client appreciation event. When a team is thankful for their clients and recognizes their value as human beings, this comes naturally and is shown in a multitude of ways.

The second is through community and charitable involvement. Businesses can be involved with local nonprofit organizations and use their influence in the community as a platform for the greater good. This is an outward display of their gratitude and appreciation for their own clients and also shows humility in serving others.

We are humbled by the opportunity to serve our community, and you, through this book.

Because of this, we have committed 100 percent of the profits from the sale of this book to benefit local charities in our own community.

PART 4

Making Your Decision

"When your values are clear to you,
making decisions becomes easier."

—ROY E. DISNEY

As we stated in the introduction of this guide, the reason for this book is simple:

To help you understand the basics of the retail financial services industry and confidently hire a wealth management team that best suits the current and future needs of your family.

In no way do we claim that this guide is fully comprehensive, or an end-all-be-all guide to hiring a wealth management team. There are a lot of options, different arrangements, and capable teams who can serve you. We hope this guide has helped enhance your understanding and that you are better equipped to navigate the decisions you will soon be making.

As we have mentioned throughout this book, we encourage you to access the resources we have built to assist you through this process. The *Pre-Meeting Checklist*, an *Advisor Interview Questionnaire*, and *Post-Meeting Scorecard* are available to download and print directly from our website at www.findingyourfinancialvisor. com. These resources are intended to help walk you through the initial discovery-and-research portion, guide you through the interviews, and rank your candidates.

The *Post-Meeting Scorecard* is intended to help rank how a team compares to another, but this is purely to help guide your decision. This guide is provided for your personal use, complementary with this book, and we encourage you to utilize these tools as you go through the decision-making process.

It is important to ensure your Five Minimum Standards are met, the interview is comprehensive and satisfactory, and that your choice of advisors ranks highly with respect to your scorecard. However, the most important factor in making your final decision is less about the brain and more about the heart.

When you find the right fit, you will feel confident, comfortable, and connected with who you choose to serve you.

You do need to capture all the key information to help you make a decision, but your gut feeling is more important than checking all the boxes.

We hope you have found this resource helpful, and you are more comfortable and confident in hiring an advisor. Please share our guide with your friends, family, and colleagues, as they pursue hiring their own advisors.

Thank you for the honor of contributing to your financial success and allowing us to be your Financial Advocate.

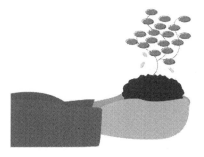

Resources

1. https://www.letsmakeaplan.org/

2. https://investmentsandwealth.org/certifications/welcome-to-cpwa

3. https://investmentsandwealth.org/certifications/welcome-to-cima

4. https://www.finra.org/about

5. https://www.sec.gov/about/what-we-do

6. https://adviserinfo.sec.gov/

7. https://brokercheck.finra.org/

8. https://www.cfp.net/ethics/code-of-ethics-and-standards-of-con-duct#practice-standards-for-the-financial-planning-process

9. Morgan Housel, *The Psychology of Money* (Hampshire, UK: Harriman House, 2020).

.

About the Authors

Our wealth management team is based in Bowling Green, Kentucky, and serves clients across the nation. Over the past two decades, we have strategically built a diverse, multigenerational team of professionals with varied specializations, designed to deliver a core-value wealth management experience. Above all else, we believe in Wisdom, Discipline, Humility, and Transparency in the wealth management process.

We have helped hundreds of clients through a wide range of life transitions, and our mission is to shed light on the biggest challenges people face when hiring a financial advisor. This book has been carefully crafted to help you confidently navigate these challenges.

Made in United States
Orlando, FL
15 September 2022

22459104R00050